In the Company of Whales

Text & Photographs by

In the Company of Whales

from the Diary of a Whale Watcher

ALEXANDRA MORTON

ORCA BOOK PUBLISHERS

First edition

Orca Book Publishers
PO Box 5626, Station B
Victoria, BC Canada
V8R 6S4

Orca Book Publishers
Box 3028, 1574 Gulf Road
Point Roberts, WA   USA
98281

Canadian Cataloguing in Publication Data
Morton, Alexandra, 1957-
In the company of whales

ISBN 1-55143-000-2
1. Whales—British Columbia—Pacific Coast—
Juvenile literature. I. Title.
QLTST.C4M67 1993   j599.5'3   C93-091561-5

Design by Christine Toller
Printed in Hong Kong

All photographs by Alexandra Morton except the following:

Robin Morton — pages 7, 9, 13, 22 (bottom), 36, 60
R. Tyrrell — pages 40, 56
N. Ebell — pages 48
J. Powell — page 57

In memory of Robin Morton
father, husband, best friend and teacher

~

Dedicated to my brothers Wade and Lloyd,
my sisters Woodleigh and Suzanne,
my parents Barbara and Earl
and my son Jarret
with whom I cherish the strong bonds of family.

Introduction

When I first arrived in British Columbia I did not expect to spend the rest of my life here. My intention was to visit for a few summers, study whales and return each winter to a job in a city.

I had always liked the idea of living in the wilderness, but I had never actually experienced it, so there were many surprises. All the beautiful films and pictures didn't prepare me for how itchy, soggy and dirty it could be. But from the first day I arrived, I was sure that I had finally found my place on this planet. I cannot explain why, but, after travelling to many places, I just knew that this was where I wanted to stay. The reason I came to British Columbia was to find one particular family of killer whales; I stayed because I fell in love with the place.

The first killer whales or orca that I came across were in a small pool near Los Angeles. When I first met them I thought they were slow, uninteresting creatures. At that time, 1978, I was studying communication among the quick, playful bottle-nosed dolphins in another tank at Marineland of the Pacific. I was trying to figure out their language and I thought a good way to do that might be to keep track of everything they did and every sound they made. Then on my computer I could match the two. As everyone knows, it is not easy to figure out what a person is saying in another language. It is even more difficult to figure out what another species is saying! The big trouble was that the eleven dolphins in that tank moved so fast I simply could not describe every move they made.

By comparison the killer whales seemed quite uninteresting. Whenever I happened to pass their tank, Orky, the male, was usually just floating on the surface, his flopped-over dorsal fin resembling an old car tire. The female, Corky, was always moving, circling the tank again and again. Some of the children who came to see her thought she was a machine because she always came up in the same spot to breathe. I never watched them for long.

Then one day Corky surprised all of us by having a baby. No one knew she was pregnant until the tiny tail of her calf appeared. The curator of the park asked me to bring my underwater listening equipment from the dolphin tank and record the sounds of the new baby. I was very happy to be asked and wondered what a baby killer whale would sound like. I was so interested I stayed awake for most of three days, napping in my chair whenever the whales were quiet, which was not often. Whales do not sleep like us and can stay awake all night. The baby made a raspy little cry that was not very different from a human baby's cry.

What I witnessed at the aquarium was very sad. Corky did not know how to take care of her baby. We guessed that she had not been old enough to learn how to be a mother before she was captured. The baby never nursed, though he tried.

Within a few days the little whale died. My home was two hours from the aquarium and I cried the whole way. But, as a result of this experience, I decided that the slower moving killer whales would be easier to study than the dolphins. At least my eyes and mouth could keep up with them.

I spent two years studying Orky and Corky on a part-time basis. Every month I spent twelve hours watching them. One month I spent the day from 6AM to 6PM watching the whales and the next month I spent the night from 6PM to 6AM. I did this so I could find out if they did different things at night. I recorded their sounds and wrote down everything I saw.

I enjoyed being with the whales at night best because there were no other people around. They played whale games and were always up to something new. And they were certainly not at all boring! They did

strange things I didn't understand, like greeting the sunrise with their mouths open and tongues stuck out!

At the end of the two years Corky had another baby and it died too. Watching baby whales die was too sad for me, so I decided to try studying whales in the wild.

Each family of killer whales speaks a slightly different language, called a dialect. No one knows why they do this, but some of us think it is so they don't get confused and lost when many families travel together. Imagine you are in a dark field with your family and a lot of other people. If there was something about your family's speech that set it apart from the rest, it would be easier for your mother or father to tell you when it was time to go. Underwater it is murky and often very dark, and it would be easy for a whale to get separated from its family.

Having spent two years learning Corky's family dialect, I didn't want to start all over again with a new language, so I decided to try and find her family. I knew that Dr. Mike Bigg, one of the top research scientists in the field, had counted and photographed almost all the families of whales on the west coast, so I called him. I was nervous because he was so famous and I was only twenty years old. I worried that he would think I was just a kid and not want to talk to me. But my fears were unfounded. Dr. Bigg was very nice and told me what I needed to know. He sent me pictures of Corky's family and said that the best place to look for them was off the east coast of Vancouver Island near Alert Bay during the month of August.

I spent the next few months making lists of what I would need for this exciting expedition. I saved enough money to buy an inflatable boat and practised going out in it. When the time came, I piled pots and pans, tent, boat, engine, food, tape recorder, camera, and lots of warm clothes into the back of my pickup truck. And off I went. It took me three days to drive from San Diego to Alert Bay.

Due to Dr. Bigg's help and lots of luck I found the whales I was looking for the very first day. In actual fact, they found me. I was still

tied to the dock in Alert Bay when I heard them blowing. It was sunset and they looked very beautiful. The ocean was golden and their blows looked silver. It felt like the beginning of my life. I wished with all my heart that I could have brought Corky with me to see her family again.

I was raised in Connecticut in the mountains of New England, a place very different from the island I live on now. When I first moved here, there was a great deal I had to learn about the ocean and the forest. At first I was very brave. I didn't really know anything about the dangers involved, so I wasn't afraid. Then experience taught me otherwise. I felt the tremendous power of big storms on the ocean. I hit a rock and nearly sank my boat. One day a bear tried to push down the side of my house. When I first heard wolves howling at night, I thought for sure I was going to be attacked. And when my boat broke down in the middle of nowhere, I thought I was going to drift away and be lost forever. But out of fear comes respect, and I eventually learned to understand and respect the power of the natural environment.

Not long after I moved to Alert Bay I met Robin Morton, a filmmaker, and later we were married and began to work together. I felt very safe with Robin, because no matter how bad things got, he always figured out what to do. If the boat broke down, he fixed it. If we got lost, he found the way. I could generally just follow his instructions and take care of our baby.

Then one terrible afternoon Robin's diving equipment failed and he drowned. I did not know it was possible to feel that sad. I didn't want to talk to anybody or do anything. I didn't even want to get up in the morning. Fortunately there was one person who needed me. One person who made me get up and keep going and that was my son Jarret.

And so I had two choices. I could abandon my work and the life I had come to love, or I could learn to live independently with my son, who was four years old. I chose to stay where I was.

When I think back now to the many mistakes I made, I have to laugh. In the beginning I couldn't even split a piece of firewood properly. When the axe got stuck in a round of wood I didn't know how to get it out and broke the handle. When I first used a chainsaw, I

felt like I was holding a snarling beast by the tail and that at any second it might turn and rip my leg off. If a twig snapped in the bushes at night, I imagined a Sasquatch might be out there. I couldn't even manage to tie up my boat properly and it was lost in a storm, along with Jarret's Lego set. But two things helped me get through that part of my life: my neighbours and my love of the wilderness.

Someone taught me how to handle a chainsaw. I thought women weren't strong enough for this kind of thing, but when I saw that a friend, Joannie, could do it, I knew it was possible. Another person kept repairing my engine and finally I learned to do some of it myself. There is no electricity where we live, so I had to learn how to keep a generator running as well. I was shown how to fire a rifle, and while I have never had to use it, I no longer have to fear bears pushing down the side of my house. Everyone laughed at me for being afraid of wolves, so I gave that up. Storms still scare me on the water, but I go out anyway. I have learned to watch the weather, trying to read the clouds and water, so I know when to head for shelter. Because of my experiences, I now feel that I can handle most of what comes my way. And if I can't, I ask for help.

Jarret has grown up in the wilderness. I know I would have liked to have lived here when I was a child. When he was born, his father and I lived on a boat. Many people said that was no place to raise a child, but Jarret thought it was great. All the furniture was nailed to the floor, so he never had to worry about breaking things. And everywhere we went he had all his toys and his own little bunk. His bed was a cosy little cupboard where the charts had been stored!

Next we lived in a floathouse, which is a regular house built on a raft of logs. The number one rule on a floathouse is that all children have to wear their lifejacket every time they step out the door. The logs get slimy and slippery and if they fell in between two logs it would be very hard to find the surface again. The children here get used to their lifejackets; sometimes they even forget to take them off when they are in town.

Jarret's school has one room, one teacher and eight students. We don't have a schoolbus, we have a schoolboat. When the class goes ice skating,

everyone gets up in the dark and rides on a fishboat for three hours to get to Port McNeill. One day their teacher came in after recess and took the students out to see a pod of dolphins that were nearby. Even the teacher's dog went. When the principal visits, he sometimes arrives in a helicopter. Although many things are different, the school work is the same. Homework must get done and everyone looks forward to weekends.

Jarret and I lived in our floathouse until we asked a neighbour to pull it up onto some land that we bought. The house was very heavy and broke the cable twice. It had to stay half on the beach and half on land for one night and the tide came up inside. The water helped clean up all the broken jam, pickle and salmon jars that had crashed to the floor when the cable broke. The next day it was pulled all the way up. Now we have a garden and Jarret has forts and a treehouse. Our two dogs like it better on land than on the float.

Our community is very small with only about fifty people, but we do have a post office. The mail arrives three times a week by sea plane.

When I give my address, people always want to know what street I live on. When I tell them we don't have any streets, they can't believe it and I have to explain that everyone gets around by boat. On Halloween a boat takes all the children trick or treating. Another boat brings us propane and gas. One advantage we have is that we never have to wait for a snow plough to clear the roads, although one time there was so much ice on the water that I couldn't get Jarret to the school dock. Sometimes we have to miss things because there is too much wind to go out in the boat, but generally living in an isolated community is a lot of fun.

I am very happy that we decided to stay in Simoom Sound. I think that what I have learned about the whales that pass through here is very important. To learn about a wild animal a scientist has to learn to live near them. Many other people are doing this with chimpanzees, elephants, wolves, lions and other species.

All the plants and animals in an area fit together like a puzzle. If you have only one piece, like a whale in a tank, you really can't see how it fits into the whole picture. This kind of puzzle is called an ecosystem, and it is amazing to see how well everything works together. It is very important to learn as much as possible about ecosystems so that we humans can learn to fit into the puzzle without destroying it. It is my hope that some who read this will go on to study and learn new things about ecosystems that I can read about when I am an old woman. I look forward to that.

This book is about the many things the whales have taught me, and about some of the questions I have not yet found answers to. It is also about just living near whales and trying to fit in.

Alexandra Morton
Simoom Sound, B.C.

RESIDENTS

A4 Pod

A11
Yakat
(F: 1958)

A24
Kelsey
(F: 1967)

A35
Skagit
(F: 1974)

A13
Skeena
(M: 1978)

A48
Siwiti
(M: 1983)

A56
Nahwitti
(1990)

A45
Sutlej
(F: 1983)

A49
(1985 – 87)

A53
Scylla
(1988)

A52
Kiltik
(1987)

A59
Racey
(1990)

A58
Surf
(1992)

A12 Subpod

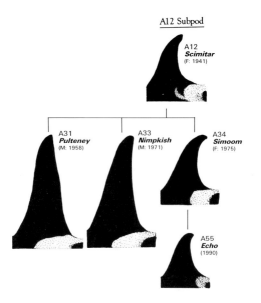

A12
Scimitar
(F: 1941)

A31
Pulteney
(M: 1958)

A33
Nimpkish
(M: 1971)

A34
Simoom
(F: 1975)

A55
Echo
(1990)

A5 Pod

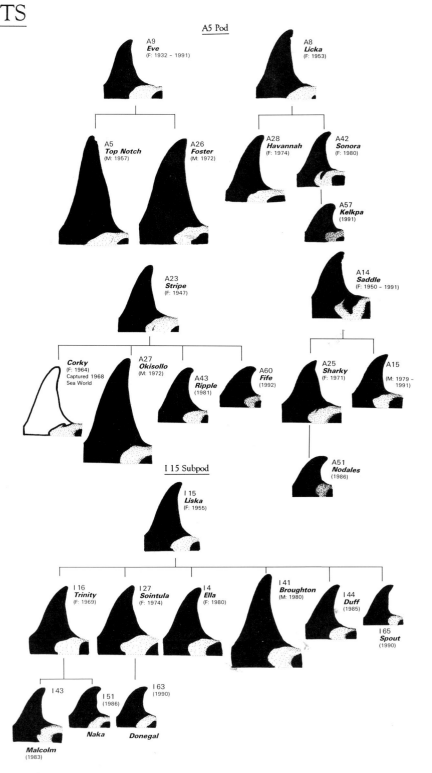

A9
Eve
(F: 1932 – 1991)

A8
Licka
(F: 1953)

A5
Top Notch
(M: 1957)

A26
Foster
(M: 1972)

A28
Havannah
(F: 1974)

A42
Sonora
(F: 1980)

A57
Kelkpa
(1991)

A23
Stripe
(F: 1947)

A14
Saddle
(F: 1950 – 1991)

Corky
(F: 1964)
Captured 1968
Sea World

A27
Okisollo
(M: 1972)

A43
Ripple
(1981)

A60
Fife
(1992)

A25
Sharky
(F: 1971)

A15
(M: 1979 –
1991)

A51
Nodales
(1986)

I 15 Subpod

I 15
Liska
(F: 1955)

I 16
Trinity
(F: 1969)

I 27
Sointula
(F: 1974)

I 4
Ella
(F: 1980)

I 41
Broughton
(M: 1980)

I 44
Duff
(1985)

I 65
Spout
(1990)

I 43
Malcolm
(1983)

I 51
(1986)
Naka

I 63
(1990)
Donegal

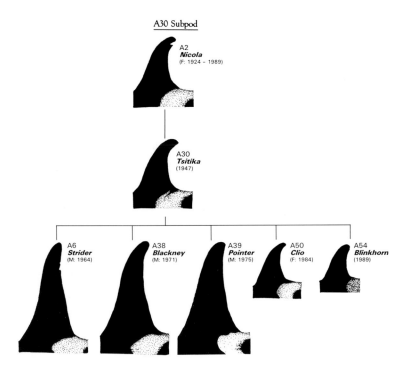

A30 Subpod

A2
Nicola
(F: 1924 – 1989)

A30
Tsitika
(1947)

A6
Strider
(M: 1964)

A38
Blackney
(M: 1971)

A39
Pointer
(M: 1975)

A50
Clio
(F: 1984)

A54
Blinkhorn
(1989)

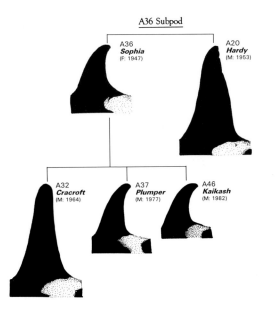

A36 Subpod

A36
Sophia
(F: 1947)

A20
Hardy
(M: 1953)

A32
Cracroft
(M: 1964)

A37
Plumper
(M: 1977)

A46
Kaikash
(M: 1982)

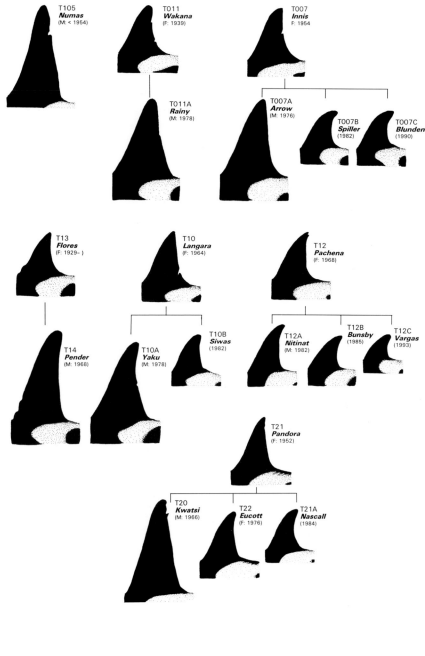

T105
Numas
(M: < 1954)

T011
Wakana
(F: 1939)

T007
Innis
F: 1954

T011A
Rainy
(M: 1978)

T007A
Arrow
(M: 1976)

T007B
Spiller
(1982)

T007C
Blunden
(1990)

T13
Flores
(F: 1929–)

T10
Langara
(F: 1964)

T12
Pachena
(F: 1968)

T14
Pender
(M: 1968)

T10A
Yaku
(M: 1978)

T10B
Siwas
(1982)

T12A
Nitinat
(M: 1982)

T12B
Bunsby
(1985)

T12C
Vargas
(1993)

T21
Pandora
(F: 1952)

T20
Kwatsi
(M: 1966)

T22
Eucott
(F: 1976)

T21A
Nascall
(1984)

Spring

18 June

0600 — The morning is perfect for spotting whale blows. The wind is just a light northern ripple and the sky is clear. As we head north I scan the horizon for blows, while Jarret sleeps in his bunk in the bow. No porpoise spotted, but there are salmon jumping and lots of birds. I don't know if I'll find whales, but I know that a good place to look at this time of year is in the inlets. Salmon follow the herring and eulachon (a little fish rich in oil, known to the natives as candlefish), which come into the inlets to spawn. Afterwards the salmon slowly head out to sea again and the whales show up to meet them.

0740 — Drop the hydrophone. At first all I hear is the snapping of shrimp and the strange little chirps that I hear only in the inlets. My underwater microphone, called a hydrophone, allows me to hear beneath the surface. Above water all may be quiet, but underwater I can hear rock cod grunting, otters piping, many unidentified sounds like the little chirps, and, of course, the calls of killer whales. The whales can be very loud and heard ten miles away if there are not too many boat engines drowning them out. Often the best way to find whales is by listening for them.

Once I have located whales with the hydrophone, I can turn on my tape recorder and record their sounds. I can only hear when the boat is stopped, because the sound of the boat engine drowns out everything else. There is also the danger of tangling the hydrophone cord in the propeller. I have lost two that way!

0955 — Faint whale calls come over the hydrophone.

1030 — Spot blows spread across the inlet, heading in. It's A1 pod, with granny in the lead. Nicola is the grandmother in this pod and she is generally out ahead. Close behind her is the adult male, Hardy. At this time of year the melting glaciers turn the inlet waters pale green and against it the whales look blacker than ever. All the whales seem in high

> **The 24-hour Clock**
>
> Scientists record time according to a twenty-four-hour clock. Six o'clock in the morning is written as 0600; four fifteen in the afternoon is 1615. To convert times after noon to the regular clock, simply subtract twelve hours.

How We Can Tell Killer Whales Apart

Dr. Bigg was the first person to discover that each killer whale looks different. Before he noticed this, scientists studying other kinds of whales and dolphins made a mark on them so they would be able to tell them apart. Dr. Bigg and his colleagues took hundreds of pictures of whales and then examined each negative through a special microscope. Before long he noticed that there were two ways to tell killer whales apart.

First, each dorsal fin, which is the fin that comes up from their back, is generally distinctive. Some fins are straighter than others or have cuts or tears in them. Some are very curved and so on. The other part of the whale to look at is the saddle, which is the grey patch behind and under the dorsal fin. The saddle is a lot like our fingerprints, because no two are exactly the same. Some look like a check mark, others are just a big bulge. Some have little black fingers that stick out or in. And some have deep scratches or swirls in them.

Whales get new marks and young whales' fins change as they grow. So we have to keep taking good pictures as the whales change, and keep photo records on any new ways to tell them apart.

spirits as they fish. Baby Clio is close to her mother, Tsitika, while her older brothers, Strider, Blackney and Pointer, are out in the middle. They are cruising. With just the tips of their dorsal fins showing they look like sharks as they zig-zag up the inlet.

1355 — The pod turns. I can't understand why they did not want to finish their trip to the end of the inlet. Nicola and Hardy are in the lead with the rest of the pod in a tight line behind them.

1430 — The whales speed up. The wind has picked up and they look quite spectacular heading into the waves. But what is the rush? I am confused. One minute everyone is fishing and the next they're intent on getting out of there! I ask Jarret to keep an eye out the back to see if there could be something behind us in pursuit.

1530 — Now I am really confused. Hardy is out in front putting on some kind of display. He is moving in a circle, lunging out of the water, waving his pectoral fin, fluke slapping, spyhopping and making sputtering noises on the surface. The rest of the family is gathered in a line behind him floating quietly. What is going on?

1545 — Jarret spots another pod of whales coming towards us. There is a whale in the lead behaving just like Hardy. I have never seen anything like this and wonder what I am witnessing. Is this a stand-off? Will I see my first whale fight? I have never heard of anyone seeing killer whales fight. I put the hydrophone back in the water, pull my camera out of its case, set the light meter and get ready to record the event.

1600 — The lead whale in the approaching group is the adult male Top Notch. The pod is A5. Top Notch is closely followed by his brother Foster and their mother Eve. I have not seen this pod since last winter and by the looks of things neither has Hardy. Top Notch and Hardy are rubbing along each other and are soon joined by Eve, Nicola and the young female, Sharky.

The whales are so gentle with one another! I guess that what I am witnessing is a spring reunion. Meetings between killer whales that know each other are always affectionate, but the display by the males is rare and I believe might signal the end of a long separation. These two families are close relatives, somewhere not too far back in their family trees they must share a great grandmother. We know this because the calls they use are so similar.

As sunset approaches Jarret and I leave these two families once again heading into the inlets. They seem to have fallen asleep together and their blows are rising in unison.

Top-notch

How Whales Get Their Names

Every killer whale of the northwest coast of North America has been given an alpha-numeric code. Alpha-numeric means a letter and number. The letter tells us what pod the whale is from; the number indicates the individual whale. These codes were first given to the whales by Dr. Michael Bigg who began killer whale research in this area in the early 1970s.

Codes are easier to use for a scientist using a computer to keep track of information, but they are not necessarily the easiest way for people to keep track of whales. Over the years the whales have also been given names. Often these names refer to a mark or shape on the whale. For example: A25 is Sharky, because her fin resembles a shark fin; A2 was Nicola, because she had a big nick in her fin; A12 is Scimitar because her fin resembles a kind of sword, and A14 was known as Saddle because the grey patch behind her dorsal fin (known as a saddle) was so different from the other whales' patches. Other whales have been given the names of places where they have been sighted.

Whales and Dolphins Found off the West Coast of North America

When people think of whales on the west coast, they most often think of killer whales or Gray whales, but there are, in fact, seven species of cetaceans (whales, dolphins and porpoises) commonly found in the region: harbour porpoise, Dall porpoise, Pacific white-sided dolphins, killer whales, Minke whales, Gray whales and humpback whales.

The smallest is the harbour porpoise (*Phocoena phocoena*), which is only about 1.8 m (5.8 ft) long and weighs about 90 kg (200 lb). This shy, little grey porpoise eats herring and lives in shallow water, usually close to shore.

Next smallest are the Dall porpoise (*Phocoenoides dalli*), which are black and white and grow to be 2.2 m (7 ft) and 200 kg (440 lb). When I get a radio call from someone saying they see a whole pod of baby killer whales, I know they are looking at Dall porpoise. They like to bowride, but I have never seen them leap out of the water.

Pacific white-sided dolphins (*Lagenorhynchus obliquidens*) grow to be at least 2.3 m (8 ft) and weigh 150 kg (330 lb). These white and grey striped dolphins usually live in big groups of 50 to 200. They like to bowride and often leap high out of the water. I am also doing research on this species of cetacean.

The killer whale (*Orcinus orca*) is actually the largest species of dolphin in the world. They grow to about 8 m (26 ft) and weigh as much as 8 tons. The dorsal fin of the male is much larger than the female's and grows up to 1.8 m (5.8 ft) while the female's is only about 1 m (3 ft).

The Minke whale (*Balaenoptera acutorostrata*) have baleen instead of teeth and are the smallest baleen whale in the North Pacific. The grow to 10 m (33 ft); the females are slightly bigger than the males. They are grey on top and white underneath and their pectoral fins have a white stripe on them. Their dorsal fin is small and curved. They generally live alone and eat small, schooling fish, like herring.

The Gray whale (*Eschrichtius robustus*) also has baleen but feeds by sifting through the mud for food. It grows to about 12 m (39 ft), has a mottled grey skin and no dorsal fin. They like the outside coast best and do not often come into the inlets.

Humpback whales (*Megaptera novaeangliae*) are known for the songs the males sing during the mating season. They grow to about 16 m (50 ft) and have long pectoral fins, which are the side fins attached just behind their heads. Humpbacks like to leap out of the water and sometimes surround fish with bubbles to keep them corralled so the whale can catch them. They also have baleen.

Many other species, including false killer whales, Sei whales, sperm whales (which have the largest brain on this planet), and even blue whales and fin whales can also be spotted along the west coast from time to time.

Pacific white-sided dolphins

Humpback whale

20 June

0925 — All the sea lions have left their winter haulout site and have headed west towards the summer rookeries where they will have their pups. Their rock is strangely silent. There are many rocks to choose from, but seals and sea lions have their favourites and will always return to those rocks, called haulouts, year after year.

1045 — Spot an unusually large group of five harbour porpoises with the first calf I have seen this year. Harbour porpoise are the smallest cetacean on the B.C. coast and generally travel alone or in pairs.

30 June

A whale's call booms out of the speaker in my kitchen. I listen for whales twenty-four hours a day. When I hear them I try to get to the boat as quickly as possible before they disappear. I grab my camera bag, but it seems stuck to the floor. I yank hard and the contents spill out. Another call reverberates through the small cabin, the sound too big for this little house. I scoop up a camera and a few rolls of film and dash for the boat. But it won't start. Then I hear another call just as loud. It's Nicola's pod. Finally I get the boat started and away from the dock, only to realize that I've left Jarret behind.

Then I sit up in bed. It is all just a dream!!!

WEEEEOOOOOOUUUUPPPP another call pierces the dark. I smile; this happens all the time. Whale calls come over the speaker and I dream of trying to reach them. At least I woke up this time. Groggily I switch on my flashlight and write . . .

0310 — Whale calls from house hydrophone, Nicola's pod. Calls are growing fainter gradually, they are probably headed north. With that done I lie back and listen. What are they saying to each other? I can hear loud calls, then fainter ones. Are they answering one another or just stating where they are? What do whales talk about?

Listening for Whales

While it may sound quiet above the surface of the water, there can be a lot of noise underneath. To hear underwater you need an underwater microphone, called a hydrophone. Sound travels far underwater. I have heard killer whales up to ten miles away and it is likely they can hear each other over much greater distances.

I have a hydrophone in my boat to use while I'm out on the water, and I also have one that is connected to a speaker in my house. The hydrophone is on the end of a long cable that goes out my window, down to the beach and 17 m (55 ft) out into the water, where it lies on the bottom. I leave it on all the time.

With the underwater microphone I can hear many things, like boats, shrimp and some fish. Sometimes I can hear things I can't identify. But the reason I have it on is to listen for whales and dolphins. With the hydrophone I know when they go by my house, even at night. Because the killer whale pods use different dialects, I can even tell which family is passing by. The hydrophone is an extremely useful tool for studying whales.

Photo-Identification

Photo-identification allows a scientist to tell one whale from another using photographs. Some whales have large marks in their fins, but others have almost no marks at all. To be able to tell whales apart a good photograph is necessary. The photograph must include the entire dorsal fin and the grey patch, or saddle, just behind the fin. Since a whale's saddle is different on each side, it was decided to always photograph the left side. Getting a good ID shot can be very difficult and so if we only need a picture of one side it makes the job easier.

The photograph must be in focus, have enough light on it to see all the little marks in the saddle and must be close-up in order to show the necessary detail. We use black and white film, because it does not need as much sunlight to produce a good shot.

Almost all the killer whales that come in close to the Pacific Northwest coast have been photographed. There are about 450 of them. Every year we have to update the photos. A whale's dorsal fin and saddle changes as it grows up and also as it gets new cuts and scratches. By photographing the whales each year we can keep track of these changes and look for new babies and record deaths.

Photo-identification is used on many species of whales now. However, the part of the whale photographed varies and might be the tail, head or back, depending on the species. Photos are also used to distinguish elephants by their ears, giraffes by their spots and primates by their faces. It is an extremely useful and gentle scientific technique for studying wild animals.

Summer

4 July

<u>1230</u> — Receive a call from a sport fisherman that whales are heading west and I find Nicola's pod in the lead with Sophia's A36 subpod following. Although the adults are foraging, youngsters Kaikash and Clio are playing. A subpod is a little group of whales that sometimes swims on its own and sometimes is part of a larger family. A36 pod is part of A1 pod.

The baby whales are in high spirits and are chasing each other, occasionally passing just beneath the boat. On one pass Kaikash has a frond of kelp streaming out of his mouth and Clio is trying to grab it from him. Tsitika has pulled ahead with her sons and is busy trying to fill her belly. The calves are lagging behind with Sophia who seems very tolerant of the little whales swimming in circles around and even over her.

Baby whales at play

<u>1730</u> — Tsitika and most of her family are going around the headland where I am floating, but seconds after they pass me I see them turn and head back, fast. Strider, Blackney and Pointer are close behind Tsitika.

When they get back to the point, Tsitika makes a very loud call from right beneath my boat. The needles on my tape recorder go all the way to the end of the red zone. I wonder what is wrong and then I see Clio porpoising full speed towards her mum. (When a whale moves very fast, it curves its back high out of the water to take a breath. This is called porpoising.)

I guess that, when Tsitika went around the point of land, she could no longer hear her baby and dashed back to check on her. Clio must have been concerned too, because, as soon as she heard her mother again, she dashed to her side. This makes me realize how carefully the whales listen for each other all the time. Clio could not have been out of earshot for more than a minute! With her family reunited Tsitika turns again. But now she has to put up with Clio's wild mood and quit fishing.

I caught a little pink salmon and fried it up for dinner. Jarret drove while I cooked. It's a beautiful evening and as usual the whales are responding to it.

<u>2000</u> — The sky is streaked deep red and orange with a light west wind blowing. The whales are spyhopping, floating in tight groups, porpoising and waving their flukes. The young males are chasing each other with calves close behind. The sounds are mostly whistles, gurgles and toneless little ditties. Killer whales use clicks for echolocation to "see" underwater, and calls to pass information and identity, but when they play the sounds become wild, uncontrolled, and sound just plain silly.

Echolocation

Most creatures depend more heavily on one of their senses than the others. Eagles depend most on their eyes, dogs rely on their sense of smell, and killer whales are acoustic, which means they depend on their use of sound.

Killer whales use sound to find out what lies ahead in the murky and often dark water. This is called echolocation, which means locating objects by using echoes. The whale sends out clicks one after the next. The clicks travel away from the whale until they hit something and then they bounce back. By listening to the echoes the whale can figure out what is ahead. The echo from a fish sounds different than the echo off a rock. The whale turns its head back and forth sending clicks out over a wide area. This can be compared to walking at night with a flashlight and scanning the darkness ahead.

When a whale finds something it is interested in, like a fish, it sends out shorter clicks, and more of them. This makes their "flashlight" brighter, but they "see" a smaller area. Because sound travels right through skin and flesh, a whale doesn't "see" a fish the same way as we would. Instead it "looks" right inside. Oddly enough, the brightest spot on a fish is the little air bubble in the fish's swim bladder. Whales must be able to echolocate into other whales as well and know if a female is carrying a calf or if another whale has gas.

Some scientists think that whales and dolphins can send out sounds strong enough to stun fish. A stunned fish would be slow and confused, making it much easier to catch.

Scientists have learned about echolocation from whales and bats. Now we can use this knowledge to see underwater from submarines and to look inside our own bodies.

6 July

<u>0830</u> — Spot two bucks swimming across a channel. The males swim from island to island in search of does and food. We almost never see the females swimming. Our two dogs, Golden retriever Kelsy and Jack Russell terrier Mocha, think swimming deer are far more interesting than whales! They leaned over the side of the boat watching carefully. I am amazed that deer with such slender legs can stand the very cold water.

14 July

<u>0931</u> — Spot three killer whale breaches and Dall porpoise rooster-tailing in the same location. Are the whales attacking the porpoise? Rooster-tailing is when a whale or dolphin breaks the surface going at such high speed that an arch of water sprays off their fin.

<u>0938</u> — Two Dall porpoise are foraging with Tsitika's family and there are

Dall porpoise roostertailing

Resident vs Transient Whales

There are two very different types of killer whales on the west coast of North America. These two groups behave differently, sound different, look a little different and even eat different foods. The whales we see the most often and therefore know the most about are the resident whales. They are called residents because every summer they are found in the same places. The others are called transients because we never know when or where one of these whales might turn up. Residents and transients have never been seen swimming together as one group. We think they are two separate populations, which means that they do not breed together. Here are some of the differences:

	RESIDENTS	TRANSIENTS
food	fish	mammals
pod size	6-50	1-6
dialects	differs in each pod	similar in all pods
vocalize	most of the time	rarely
fin shape	curved	pointed
travel	direct routes	wander into every bay
observed	mostly in summer	mostly in fall and spring

Much more is known about resident whales because they often stay in one area for long periods of time in the summer. This allows researchers to watch them every day for several weeks at a time. Transients are more mysterious, because they appear suddenly, might remain for a few days, and then can disappear for years. Therefore it is taking longer to collect information about them. Because my research is year-round, I have been able to collect a lot of what is known about transients.

birds in a cloud above them, indicating that the fish are near the surface. Tsitika is a fish-eater and so the porpoise are probably safe in her company. Both the whales and the porpoise are feeding on the schools of fish.

I have to keep in mind, however, that I should be prepared to see anything. I don't think Tsitika will eat a porpoise, but killer whales are constantly reminding me to expect the unexpected. Therefore I must keep my eyes and mind open and rewrite the rules as I learn them.

0956 — The porpoise leave Tsitika and Blackney and join Broughton, a young male from Liska's family of ten whales. They seem to be actually working with the whales, coming up alongside them and sweeping in arcs towards the whales. Are the swift porpoise herding the fish towards the whales? Why would they want to hunt with the whales? How do the porpoise know that these whales are interested only in fish, while other whales would be happy to make a meal of them?

Killer Whale Families

Resident killer whales live in very unusual families. When a calf is born, it will stay in its mother's pod for its whole life, even if it is a male. Most young males of other species have to leave their families, but resident male killer whales don't. A typical family consists of a granny, all her sons and daughters, and her daughter's babies. We believe fathers stay with their own families. So young whales grow up with their brothers and uncles, not their fathers. When a resident whale does not show up with its family for a year, we consider it dead.

It is harder to know the nature of the transient whale family because we are not able to study them as consistently as we do the resident population. In some cases, at least, it appears that only the oldest son stays with his mother. Transient whales are usually seen in groups of five or less, which means that they must be splitting up their families. This is probably due to the type of food they prefer. Hunting mammals might be more successful with a small group, while hunting fish might require or allow a bigger group. This is a hypothesis (a scientific guess) that has not been proven.

23 August

<u>0748</u> — Foggy and calm. The whales are headed east towards the mainland. I have identified Tsitika's and Liska's families. There is something very attractive about Liska's family. They have been dubbed the "Love Pod." Other families, in particular families with males in them, like to swim close to Liska's pod. Liska has six living offspring and three grandchildren, which is very prolific for a killer whale, but none of them are adult males. The oldest male is Broughton, who is only twelve and still has a small dorsal fin.

Although several pods might like to escort Liska, they take turns and seem very polite about the whole thing. If Scimitar's family, for example, would like to take Tsitika's place, they will float around at a distance waiting until enough space opens up. This happens while the whales are underwater. When it is time to surface again, if Scimitar and her sons have found a place alongside Liska, the others move off and wait.

<u>0832</u> — The whales have turned southeast and are in loose groups. The males are all playing except Blackney, who is travelling with Tsitika, his mum.

I have not been able to figure out why this one pod of ten members is so attractive. Is it because Liska or one of her mature daughters is ready to produce another calf? Or is it because Broughton is so much fun to play with? Half of the pod is under the age of ten and only three of them are adults, making this a very young pod.

When a pod has so many youngsters, they spend more time drifting and playing than pods that are mostly adult. Kelsy and Yakat, two adult sisters, have a family like that. I have spent entire days with them, drifting while they play gently on the surface with their calves.

<u>0907</u> — The direction is west now, but I have noticed that we are not really going anywhere. The fog is very thick, so I am happy to be going nowhere. I don't have a radar, so I can't see in the fog.

It is funny to watch a group of serious travellers like Tsitika's family trying to muster enough patience to spend a day with Liska. Four times the brothers have come up alongside Liska, blowing and diving in a determined manner. Each time I prepare to start my engine because I think the two pods are going to make a move. I wait to see which direction they will take, only to find they aren't going anywhere. The boys are the only ones who have moved. Slowly they drift back alongside Liska. I have seen this before and I've come to understand that the two pods will not likely move until Liska or a whale in her family wants to go!

1223 — Still floating, nuzzling, spyhopping and playing with kelp. I have been listening for ten minutes, but the whales are silent. Broughton is no longer participating in the play group, but all the calves and adult males, Blackney and Pointer, are very active. Strider has taken his place with Tsitika, his mum. Tsitika's sons generally make sure that one of them is with her. I have no explanation for this, because it would seem unlikely that she needs protection and they aren't there helping her catch food. This is just another one of many killer whale behaviours that tells me how tight the bond is between mother and offspring.

1700 — Finally both pods make a move to the east, against the tide. Someone must have gotten hungry and they are off to find a school of fish. I know Jarret and I are hungry as well, while "the girls," our two dogs, are very keen to hit the beach. Mocha, still a puppy, chewed the wire to the hydrophone and I'll have to repair it tonight.

Whales and the Light in the Sky

When I was studying the two captive whales, Orky and Corky, I witnessed a very interesting behaviour. Every morning just before the sun came up, they picked a place on the side of their tank, and swam up to it, opened their mouths, flicked out their tongues and squirted water. When the sun came up, I noticed that the spot the whales had chosen was exactly the spot where the sun first hit the wall. Naturally this spot moved a little each day as the sun moved along the horizon. It was interesting that the whales kept track of this and always picked the right spot.

I thought this behaviour was very strange. If the colourful sunrise was covered by a cloud the whales stopped their behaviour, until the cloud moved on. Due to the way their tank was built, they could not see the sunset. One night, however, there was lightening and the male, Orky, flicked his tongue at it and made a low groaning sound at the same time. I have no idea why they did these things, but it made me realize that whales notice events in the sky in addition to what is happening underwater.

In wild whales I have seen lots of interesting behaviours during colourful sunsets. One evening two bulls floated on their sides, head-to-tail, and held up their right pectoral fins towards the sun. My husband Robin took an amazing photograph of four whales all lined up in a row in a high spyhop. They were facing the sunset. The whales often get very playful at sunset, unfortunately just as it is getting too dark to take pictures!

25 August

0545 — Depart our anchorage. Jarret is asleep in the bow, curled up with Mocha. I have the coffee on as we speed out over the smooth water. The sunrise has made everything pink, including my boat.

0615 — Listen for whales, drifting out with the tide. Several Dall porpoise pass us hunting in the tide line. When the incoming and outgoing tides meet, they sandwich small fish, kelp, logs, even glass balls from Japan, into a long winding line. This line is like a table set for dinner and attracts birds, dolphins and whales. No calls.

0815 — Spot whales. It is Nicola's pod. They are spread out with Strider, Blackney and Pointer sweeping towards the north, Tsitika and the babies are fishing along the tide line towards me and Nicola is in the lead between the two groups.

1015 — One of the males breaches and all whales pick up speed. The pod is coming together around Nicola.

1022 — Entire pod is floating now. Strider comes up in a very high spyhop. I put the hydrophone down. I just spotted blows to the west heading in this direction. Looks like Nicola's pod is waiting to escort newcomers into their summer feeding grounds. They do this often. Without any sign that I can detect, Nicola will lead her family to the west, and there, as if by appointment, they meet another pod coming in.

It's possible that whales can hear each other from a much greater distance than I can. So while I think it is silent underwater, they might be picking up faint calls from twenty miles away. Or perhaps incoming whales wait until they are invited to approach and today Nicola was just checking the "front door."

1043 — Strider and Blackney meet the males from the other pod. They are from H pod. All the whales turn east and swim fast.

The meeting of two pods of whales that know each other is wonderful to watch. The males rush about in tight groups chasing and splashing each other. Because the pods are made up of families, the

Killer Whale Behaviour

Killer whales are very difficult to study because most of the time they are underwater where we can't see them. We have to watch behaviours on the surface carefully so we can understand what they are doing. These are a few of the behaviours we have learned about:

Sleep — Whale sleep is very different from ours. Some scientists think that whales only let half of their brain sleep at a time. When whales sleep they often line up side-by-side in a "resting line" and all breathe together. They swim so close that I think they may often be touching one another. The babies swim just behind the widest part of their mother's body, which is at her dorsal fin and in that way she can tow them in her wake. Sleeping whales seem to prefer to swim facing into the current. Current is like wind and could carry tastes like the wind carries scent. Having the current coming towards them might help a sleepy whale keep track of what is ahead.

Feeding — Feeding behaviour depends on what the whale is feeding on. In resident whales, when I see them travelling along the coast and can hear them clicking, I know they are hunting. When they find a school of fish, the clicking changes from a steady tick, tick, tick, to very quick clicks that sound just like a squeaky door being opened. The clicks are so fast that to our ears they all run together into one sound. Feeding whales will often start milling around in one place and seagulls will appear, diving to pick up the leftovers. If I look carefully I can see fish scales drifting along and little bits of the guts.

Transient whales kill harbour porpoises and seals so quickly that I generally don't know what is happening until it is over and a piece floats to the surface. It is the arrival of the birds that usually alerts me to the kill. If the whales are attacking a Dall porpoise, there is a chase; if the prey is a sea lion, there is a mighty amount of splashing.

Travel — Travelling whales are often silent, in a tight group and moving fast. This has been named "silent running." Often, however, sleep and travel are combined and the whales move slowly. Or travel can be combined with hunting and the whales stop now and then to mill about, or it is combined with play and a few whales may be racing around, while the pod is generally moving in a constant direction.

Play — There are many kinds of play, depending on which whales are involved. Calves might pull on kelp or drag around a piece of fish. Young males get very active chasing, pushing and rolling over and under each other. Transients sometimes play with a bird, by taking it underwater or batting it into the air. The more intelligent an animal is, the more its behaviour changes to fit the circumstances. This is especially true of play. That is the advantage to having a big brain; it allows a creature to adapt quickly to each situation.

Killer Whale Dialects

Dr. John Ford, a Canadian scientist, discovered that each pod of resident killer whales uses its own unique calls. Some families share calls and only have one or two of their own sounds, while other pods have no calls in common. Dr. Ford believes that the more calls that two pods share, the more closely related they are. If pods do not share any calls, they are probably not related.

Killer whales will, however, travel and hunt with pods that have a different dialect from their own, and it is likely that they understand each other to some degree. Having their own dialects may help keep families from getting separated during large gatherings.

males are the sons or brothers of the females in the pod and so they do not have any interest in fighting over them. When males from two pods get together it looks like very rough and rowdy play!

1453 — Scimitar's pod joins the group and her two sons, Pulteney and Nimpkish, join the males. The boys seem completely oblivious to where they are and what is going on around them as they tear about. Wherever they go, a boil of white water erupts.

1608 — Yakat and Kelsy move in from the south and join the edges of the growing group. Siwiti and Skeena approach the males and tag along behind. They are still a bit young to get into the middle of such rough play by so many males. If there were only one or two bulls, they might be more confident. Kelsy and her two little ones join the resting line that is forming.

Whales often have a nap an hour or so after meeting. Most of them line up side by side, with a little space between families, and begin to breathe together. If nothing interrupts them, they might sleep for twenty minutes or several hours. Today, however, the males are not interested in resting and continue to play.

2030 — The sunset is very colourful and the whales engage in sunset play. Everywhere there are whales spyhopping, and drifting on the surface. There is much vocalizing and a lot of them are nuzzling and rolling around together.

Whales definitely notice a good sunset or sunrise. I first recognized this in two whales that were taken captive from Top Notch's pod. They would flick their tongues and squirt water where the sun first touched both the wall of the tank and the water. Then they would start to play, with lots of close body contact and affection. They also squirted water at lightening!

Although whales never behave exactly the same way every time, they often become exuberant and playful when the sky turns to shades of pink and gold.

Humpback whale

26 August

<u>1045</u> — Spot a humpback whale. I take an identity photo and name her Silver, because of the light colour of her skin. The lack of scars along the back makes me think the whale is a female. The fin is hard to spot because it is so small compared to that of a killer whale; however, her blow is extremely loud. In fact it took me an hour to actually see the whale because the loud blow travelled far on the still morning, so far that by the time I heard it the whale had submerged again.

Older people who grew up in this area tell me that humpback whales lived here year-round when they were children. Then in 1951 a neighbour called the Coal Harbour Whaling Station and told the whalers about this almost tame little group of humpbacks. In a few weeks the whales were all gone. A neighbour of mine, Bill Proctor, saw eight at once lashed by their tails to the gunwales of the killing boat, *Nahmint.*

Now a few humpbacks appear around here every year and I keep

Humpback breach

hoping one will like what it finds and stay. So far, however, there are not enough humpbacks on the coast to move back into all their old haunts.

1215 — A second humpback joins Silver. This one is heavily scarred from his dorsal fin along his back towards his flukes. He raises his tail nicely, so I get his ID shot and name him Nick, because of a mark on his dorsal fin. Friends of mine are studying humpback whales and if I can get a picture of the underside of the tails, they will know if they know the whale or if it is a new one.

Among other things, humpback whale researchers are trying to count the whales. Hunted almost to extinction, humpbacks were put on the endangered species list. They haven't been able to rebuild their numbers as fast as the Gray whales have, but they are slowly gaining. One day, if we keep the coastal ecosystems alive, there may be humpbacks living in the inlets again.

1545 — Nick and Silver have become very active since the westerly picked up. They breach together three times and are now side-swiping, spyhopping and continuing to breach individually. There is something about a west wind that really gets these whales going! Jarret has had to drive most of the afternoon, because it got too rough for me to steer and photograph. Every time I let go of the wheel the boat turned sideways to the wave and wanted to roll. Mocha hates rough weather and whined and bounced from seat to seat until finally she gave up and curled up with Kelsy.

"The girls"

Humpback Whales

Humpback whales have been studied by many people, so we know quite a lot about them. Pacific humpbacks migrate south in the winter to give birth in the warm waters off Mexico and Hawaii. In early spring they move north to feed along the coast of British Columbia and Alaska. They are found in other oceans as well and migrate along different routes there.

Humpbacks are also photographed for identification. When a humpback dives deep, it throws its tail up into the air. The underside of the tail or flukes is different on each whale; each has a unique pattern of black and white. So humpback researchers photograph tails. If I see a humpback, I photograph its tail and send the photo to humpback whale researchers. This helps them find out where the whales go. Many researchers in British Columbia help each other this way, which has helped our understanding of whales to grow more rapidly.

The people who grew up in the inlets where I live have told me that humpback whales were here year-round when they were young.

Yvonne Scott told me that one day when she was a little girl the schoolboat she was in couldn't get to the school until a group of humpbacks stopped leaping in front of them! Then in 1951 all were hunted by whalers. For thirty years no humpbacks were reported in the area, but now every year a few come through. I hope that one day some of them will consider this their home again.

30 August

<u>2000</u> — Spot whales. It is a pod of transients, the marine-mammal-eating group of killer whales. Langara and her offspring Yaku and Siwas cruise past where I am anchored. I follow them to the point just before the entrance to Johnstone Strait. Then Langara stops, turns upside down on the surface and slaps the water with her tail. The next time the pod surfaces they are going in the opposite direction. I go up to the point and drop my hydrophone. I hear Tsitika's pod vocalizing further down Johnstone Strait.

These two kinds of whales seem to avoid each other whenever possible. It looks to me as though Langara decided not to enter Johnstone Strait when she heard Tsitika's calls. Instead of calling to her calves, Langara signalled them with the slapping of her tail. To the calves it was a signal, but to Tsitika and her group it was just another splash. I wonder what would happen if both groups were vocal and met each other nose to nose around a point?

Fall

02 Sept

<u>0950</u> — After drifting for two hours listening for whales, I hear the little voices of Pacific white-sided dolphins. This is the earliest in the year I've heard them and to me they signal the beginning of fall.

<u>1010</u> — Jarret and Kelsey are on the bow. Kelsy is panting with excitement watching the dolphins surface only a few feet from her nose. If I run the boat at just the right speed, they surface nicely alongside and I can get pictures of their dorsal fins. Just like the killer whales, Pacific white-sided dolphins' fins are each unique. I have learned that, if I go too fast, the fins come up covered in spray and if I go too slow the dolphins get bored with me and take off. I think I know these guys. One that I named Flag is here.

<u>1123</u> — Dolphins are "popcorning" and chasing every boat that goes by. Popcorning is when a small group of three to five dolphins leaps into the air. The point of the game seems to be that all dolphins get back into the water at the same spot. So they twist and turn mid-air and re-enter the water in a tangle of dorsal fins and flukes.

Dolphins "popcorning"

<u>1155</u> — I definitely know some of these dolphins; Snaggle Tooth is here. It makes me very happy when I get to know a group of dolphins or whales and can recognize at least some of them. It is the difference between being with strangers, and with people you know. They start becoming familiar, like friends. (I have been photographing the dorsal fins of dolphins in this area since 1984.)

They are vocalizing continuously. One of the dolphins pushes my hydrophone on the end of his beak or rostrum and spirals around it. I shorten the cable to prevent him from getting caught up in it. They certainly are cheeky little fellows!

Note: I can hear the piercing sound of a seal-scaring device coming from the nearest fish farm which is four miles away. It must be extremely loud to be so audible this far away. It is designed to hurt seals' ears; I

wonder what effect it has on the dolphins and whales? Because we live so differently from whales and dolphins, we often do things without knowing their effect on the animals. The more we get to know other creatures, the more we can learn to live with them, and become good neighbours.

<u>1545</u> — Got a whale call so we are off. The dolphins have not actually gone anywhere, but have been milling about in the same place since I found them. Shot three rolls of black and white ID photos, while Jarret shot video.

<u>1614</u> — Spot four transient whales eastbound. A sprouter, two female-sized whales and a calf.

<u>1710</u> — The four whales are headed straight for a group of about seventy-five dolphins and they are silent. I don't think the dolphins know the whales are here because they are acting as silly as ever. The whales know about the dolphins, however, because the dolphins are vocalizing loudly. I want to warn the dolphins, but I must remind myself that I am an observer. And besides, how could I tell them? Part of being a scientist means standing out of the way and letting things happen. It is not always an easy thing to do and, sometimes when a creature seems helpless, I have tried to help.

<u>1747</u> — The whales cruise right past the dolphins! This is the third time I have seen the mammal-eating transient whales pass up the fat dolphins. They would seem to be the perfect meal. Dolphins are easy to find because they are noisy, large enough to be worth the effort, and seem vulnerable. But maybe they are not all that defenceless; perhaps their large numbers somehow serve to protect them?

Helping Wild Animals

It is hard to know when to help an animal in the wild. I rescued a fawn once that was swimming across a wide channel in front of a pod of whales. He was the cutest baby animal I had ever seen, with long eye lashes and pure white spots. When I lifted him into the boat, he was weak and shivering badly, so I wrapped him in a sleeping bag. I took him to a place I thought was safe and released him.

But in the end I don't know if he survived, being so young and without a mother. Maybe it would have been better to leave him to his fate. Perhaps his mother hadn't lost track of him as I suspected. In the long run it is probably best to leave a wild creature where you find it, unless you are certain you are helping.

This is especially true of baby seals. Mother seals leave their young on beaches while they go out to feed. They return to nurse them, but every year many of these adorable babies are "rescued." People think the pup has been deserted and take them to oceanariums. When the mother returns her baby is gone. Before helping wild creatures it is best to call someone who knows about them, so you can make the right decision.

Salmon

There are five species of salmon that naturally occur on the west coast: pink, sockeye, coho (also called silver), chum and spring (chinook or king). Salmon are a fascinating and complicated fish. Born in freshwater streams, they make their way to the sea, and, depending on species, spend two to seven years in the ocean. Then, by some miracle of navigation that we don't fully understand, they return to the stream where they were born. After the eggs are released into the gravel and fertilized, the spawning salmon die, their bodies providing food for bears, wolves, eagles and many other species.

 At every stage of their life cycle salmon feed other forms of life, so they are very important to the ecosystem of the Pacific northwest. Wherever they go, they form a river of life. We need to be very careful that we don't lose them.

16 September

<u>1300</u> — Spot Eve, Licka, Saddle, Stripe and their families travelling northwest. They are spread out, foraging, with the males, Top Notch and Foster, a half kilometre away but still abreast of the pod. Jarret is back in school today and so it is just "the girls" and I in the boat.

<u>1445</u> — I spot southbound whales. It is H pod. The two pods mingle and repeatedly alter their direction of travel, making their course erratic, unpredictable and difficult to follow.

<u>1510</u> — The whales are generally moving towards the northwest. There is a dense fog bank lying in that direction and I want to make sure I don't get caught in it. Unwisely, I do not have a compass on board and, if the fog surrounds me, it will be almost impossible to know which way to go. Every few minutes I check how close the wall of grey has come. The soft edges of a fog bank make this difficult, but it is definitely rolling towards me.

<u>1630</u> — The whales are foraging in a tide line. At this time of year there are runs of coho and chum salmon flooding in with each tide and the whales seem to have found a school.

<u>1710</u> — Whales are still widespread across the sound, in small groups of two's and three's. The bulls from the two pods were close together, but I have lost track of them as they are in the fog now. Occasionally I can hear their louder male blows. As I look up from writing this, I find that the fog has swept over me too. I have waited too long! The evening, which was sunny and warm, has instantly become damp and cold, and I have no idea which way to go. I feel lost and disoriented. One direction will take me home, the opposite leads out towards the open ocean. To make matters worse, as I drift the dull roar of a luxury liner starts to grow louder over the hydrophone. I am sitting in a shipping lane and, at the high speed the liners travel, the fog could be pierced by a gigantic bow at any minute.

44

I can feel panic rising up through my body like fire. I keep thinking, *How am I going to get out of this one? What is the right thing to do? I've got to come up with something before that ship gets here.* Only one direction can be "right" — out of harm's way and towards home. In the glassy calm water there isn't even a wave pattern to follow. This is one of the most terrifying moments in my life.

The sense of panic is tingling along my scalp, threatening to take over, when WHHOOOOSH Eve, Licka, Top Notch and the other whales of A5 pod surface close beside me. I want to reach out and hug them. They are safety itself! I know that they are not going to be run down by the ship. All I have to do is stick with these whales and I'll be safe. Then it strikes me that in this thick fog I will lose them on their next dive.

Three minutes pass and then there they are again, their dorsal fins spread like a fan beside my boat. As they dive Saddle and her two young, Sharky and her brother, angle beneath me. I shift into neutral gear; they are so close I do not want the spinning propeller to hurt them. Every time they blow I think, *Oh, thank you for not deserting me.* I try to match their course. While they are down, I glance behind to make sure my wake is as straight as possible. In the fog it is easy to go in a circle without knowing it.

After twenty minutes the fog looks a little different ahead. Yes, I decide, it is becoming clearer. Suddenly I can see a tree on a rocky little islet. The whales are down and I speed towards the islet. In seconds I burst out of the grey into a beautiful sunset.

I am surprised when I recognize where I am. I thought we had been going in the opposite direction. All day the whales had been moving northwest, but, while they were with me, we had apparently turned and cruised in a southeast direction. I wait for them to re-appear, but they never do. I hear their blows once and then they are gone. Had they turned around just for me? Did they intentionally help me? Was that even possible?

All in all this has been a very confusing day, and one I shall always remember. While it left me with many questions, I did learn one lesson that I have never forgotten: always carry a compass!

Whale Ears

Whales do not have an external ear like most other mammals. Sound waves travelling through water, which is much denser than air, will travel through all things as dense as water. Living creatures are made up mostly of water, so sound waves travelling in water go right through fish and whale skin. For this reason whale ears have no external flaps. Sounds can travel right into their heads.

However, whales still need something to direct the sound waves to their internal ears. On land the bigger the external ear the better the creature can hear. Elephants can hear each other for miles because they have enormous ears. So whales, who also communicate over long distances, need something large to receive sounds. Scientists now believe that whales pick up sound with their lower jaws. The lower jaw or mandible is specially designed as a sound receiver.

Can Whales Smell?

Whales do not have a nose. What was their nose slowly drifted backwards to the top of their head and became a blowhole. Being able to breathe out of the top of their head means that whales do not have to lift their head up out of the water every time they breathe. Instead they can roll smoothly and use less energy.

However, not only did whales lose their nose, they also lost the part of their brain used to sort out smells. This part is called the olfactory bulb and it is missing in whale brains. They can taste though, and we believe that their tongues are very sensitive. It is possible that they can taste schools of fish, freshwater or the pollution we sometimes dump in the ocean.

22 September

Today I "spoke" to a whale! I think he knew what I said, although I am not entirely sure I know what I said. I have noticed that the whales that use Tsitika's dialect often begin their "conversations" with a particular call. It sounds a little like a bullet ricocheting in the old western movies. One whale makes it, then, if the other wants to "talk," it will make the sound as well. After going back and forth with that one call, they start using other sounds. I imagine the ricocheting call says, "Hello, this is me, want to talk?" or some whale version of that.

I wondered what a whale would do if I made his sounds, and I knew this sound best. So today, when Hardy surfaced close to the boat and had his blowhole open, I cupped my hands and yelled "piiittuuuuuu." Hardy, Tsitika and the rest of her family came right over, spyhopping beside the boat and passing closely beneath us. They seemed intensely interested in what was in my boat.

I was thrilled to think I had made a sound that possibly meant something to them. Killer whales are known for being aloof, not showing any sign of interest in most human activities and so this was a big response. While we are not supposed to be able to talk to animals, I suspect there are a lot of people capable of it to some degree. I heard Jane Goodall speak once and she began her lecture with an incredibly spine-tingling chimpanzee quote!

26 September

<u>1130</u> — Spot transients Flores and Pender. The deep scars on the forward edge of their dorsal fins make them easy to recognize.

<u>1206</u> — Mother and son pursued a Dall porpoise together. They came at it from opposite sides rooster-tailing at high speed. The porpoise, however, zig-zagged an erratic course and escaped. Dall porpoise definitely know which whales to flee from and which they can swim with.

10 October

<u>1026</u> A prawn fishing vessel reports whales in the inlet. I grab my camera bag and recording gear, which I keep packed and ready by the door for radio calls like this. Jarret decides to stay at a friend's, so the girls and I head out.

<u>1049</u> — I encounter all of the A pods. There are thirty-six whales and they are all close relatives of Tsitika, Eve, Hardy and Siwiti. The whales fill the channel, with a large group of females on the north side, and smaller groups of males and juveniles across on the south side. Whales are floating, slapping and spyhopping. Very little progress is being made during the dives.

<u>1115</u> — All whales disappear. I was moving from group to group trying to account for all the whales, as this might be the last time I will see them until next spring. Suddenly they are all gone.

<u>1119</u> — I spot them again. They are all along the south side of the channel in single file. The calves are tight with their mothers, the sons flanking the females.

<u>1123</u> — As they reach a large bay, the leaders turn tightly into it and the others pour in behind them. Eve, along with the males, Top Notch, Foster and Hardy, sweeps along the back of the bay, while all the other whales line up abreast. Each time the line of whales surfaces they are pointing in a different direction. They are making "F1" calls (a sound they make when their movements are highly synchronized) and a deep grunting noise that I have never recorded before. They are also jaw-clapping, an aggressive sound that resembles two pieces of wood being hit hard together. I have never seen this behaviour before, or anything even resembling it. I have no idea what is going on.

<u>1142</u> — As suddenly as it began, it is over. The line-up has broken into little family subgroups and they are all following Eve out of the bay.

<u>1151</u> — I move my boat out into the channel again, shut down to record and immediately hear whale blows on the far, north side. I put the binoculars on them, thinking, how could anyone have gotten to the other side so quickly? But it is not any of the A clan whales. It is Pandora, Kwatsi, Eucott and a new calf, members of the transient race. They are travelling in the opposite direction close up against the north shore.

Eve leads her relatives out of the bay as soon as the transients pass. Although I cannot hear any calls from Pandora's pod, they must have been vocal earlier. The A clan whales may have quit their playful activities because they heard the transient calls and then moved to the south shore to avoid them. While moving into the bay seems a fearful response, many of their sounds could be labelled as aggressive, particularly the jaw claps.

If there had been a bay on the north shore, would Pandora have led her family into it? Is Eve's pod afraid of the mammal-eaters, or are they simply strangers to be avoided? Baby whales grow up socializing with certain pods and never come in contact with others, even though they travel the same waters. Some families are bound together by tradition, while others have no contact with each other. I still do not know why the residents and transients don't mingle, but I now know that is not by coincidence that I have never seen the two groups together.

It feels like I have witnessed the changing of the guard. Summer is resident killer whale season, while winter and spring is transient time. Occasionally there is some crossover, because killer whales are never completely predictable.

22 October

<u>1030</u> — Spot whales from the house. Jarret is in school, so I head out alone. I count eleven whales, split into two groups. They are transients. Eleven is a very large group for these whales. I generally see only four or five at a time. Kwatsi and Pandora are here. Arrow and his mother Innis are here as well, but the others are strangers.

<u>1141</u> — No matter what I do I cannot get alongside the strangers to get a good look or photograph.

<u>1340</u> — Kwatsi, in the lead, stops by the waterfall and floats. All the others join him in a tight group. They are breathing every twenty to forty seconds, which is very rapid for whales.

<u>1350</u> — They have drifted up to a point just outside a large bay and continue to breathe frequently.

<u>1400</u> — All whales make a deep dive. When whales dive deep, they show more of their back, often right down to their tail. I have started the stopwatch and I am going to move the boat into the middle of the bay.

<u>1415</u> — Fifteen minutes passes — the longest dive time that I have yet recorded. I begin to think I have been given the slip. Then suddenly a wall of white water erupts in the distance and I can hear a few faint calls. The whales are attacking at least three sea lions. I want to get closer, but for two reasons I decide to stay put and watch through binoculars. First, no one that I know of has recorded a sea lion kill from beginning to end in such quiet conditions. Second, the thought of a 2,000-pound sea lion leaping into my 1700-pound boat to escape the whales is horrific! I stay put.

<u>1435</u> — The calls suddenly become loud and I turn to see who is coming up behind me, but there are no whales there. Transients vocalize so softly their sounds have been described as "murmurs." But apparently once they have their prey immobilized, they turn up the volume.

Over time killer whales have probably learned that if their prey can hear them, they will avoid them. But if the whales whisper or murmur, seals and sea lions in the next bay won't be alerted.

A killer whale attack is made up of high speed passes during which the whales try to land a blow while not getting bitten. Sea lions have huge canines and are an aggressive and powerful animal. Many transients bear deep scars which are probably made at times like this.

The whales are striking the lions with their flukes and heads, as well as leaping on them and flipping them into the air.

<u>1515</u> — The whales are now diving repeatedly in the same place and floating between dives. I can no longer see any sign of the sea lions. The whales must be feeding. It has taken an hour to make the kill. I had no idea it was such an effort for a killer whale to make a meal of a Stellar sea lion. I have seen films and photos of killer whales and sea lions interacting, but, until I saw it for myself, I really had no idea what was involved. Both animals are immensely powerful. My boat, which used to feel fairly big, now seems flimsy.

29 November

1015 — I receive a call from an artist on a nearby island who tells me a dead killer whale has washed up on a beach near his home. Finding dead killer whales is very rare. Generally they just disappear and we never know what has happened to them. Finding the body means we can determine what killed this whale. Was it pollution, natural causes, or something else? We can also learn something about what kind of life the whale had, what it ate recently and, if it's a female, how many babies she has had. I ask my friend to describe the whale and his accurate memory for detail leaves little doubt; it is Eve.

I call the Biological Station and they organize a team to recover the body and do a full autopsy. A museum requests the skeleton. It makes me sad to think that Eve is dead. She was a leader, not only of her own pod, but also of any pod that swam with her. She had deep scoops in her back, possibly made by a boat years ago when she was a calf. She left two sons, but no daughters. I head out to assist with the autopsy.

Doing a Whale Autopsy

An autopsy is the examination of a dead body. There is a lot of useful information that can be gathered in this way. If the body is fresh, we can learn what the animal ate, what it died of, how old it is, if it had any diseases, if it had any babies and if any pollutants collected in its body. Scientist used to kill animals to study them, but now we collect most information by watching them while they are alive, and study their bodies only after they have died. It is very important to let scientists know if you find a dead wild animal. If it is on a beach, tie it to a tree or boulder so that it will not be lost to a high tide.

Cutting up dead whales is a very smelly business. I made the mistake of wearing boots with leather tops at an autopsy. Afterwards I had to throw them away, as nothing would rid them of the sickening odour. And the dogs, who seemed to find the process very interesting, had to have baths for days afterwards and nobody wanted them around!

Winter

18 December

<u>0640</u> — Top Notch and Foster were on the hydrophone last night at 2330. Since their mother's death, they have been spotted several times, always in the general vicinity of where Eve washed ashore. The rest of the clan has moved on, but the brothers remain behind. Among killer whales it appears that males who are left without any sisters never seem to enjoy tight family bonds again. They will wander among the families of their aunts or cousins.

01 January

<u>0910</u> — Encounter two pods of transients, Langara and her two calves, Yaku and Siwas, and Wakana and her young son, Rainy. Langara and Wakana are in serious pursuit of something in a kelp bed, but the three youngsters come towards our boat as we approach. They seem excited, surfacing high out of the water and moving fast. When they get close to the boat, they all dive. I thought they had moved past us, but, when they reappear, they have surrounded the boat. Yaku and Rainy have sandwiched us and little Siwas surfaces just off the bow.

Instantly I feel corralled. I don't feel at all safe in my little Zodiac. This situation reminds me of a film I saw of killer whales attacking a blue whale. Their first move was to tightly surround their prey.

The three whales dive at the same time, and again I think they have left. But seconds later Yaku surfaces close to our port side and Rainy comes up almost right beneath the starboard pontoon of the Zodiac. He then swims on the surface keeping his back in contact with the boat, pushing us into Yaku on our left.

I don't want to play this game, so I pull the throttle back into neutral and coast to a stop. If a whale's tail were to hit the spinning propeller, there is a good chance it would be cut deeply. And we might all end up hurt. As the three young whales porpoise away exuberantly, my mind is racing. Why had they done this? Were they simply testing the power of my craft? Why weren't the two females involved? I decide it must have been play, because only the young whales were involved. I just happened to come along when these youngsters were in a particularly rambunctious mood. Like play in all adolescent mammals, however, this is part of the learning process. Rainy now knew how powerful I was — or wasn't — and what my boat felt like. I am glad he tried it on me, because he's learned that I will not hurt him.

29 January

<u>1015</u> — It is blowing hurricane force. The trees are swinging in circles and the house vibrates every time a big gust hits. Spot a lone male killer whale in front of my house.

1850 — For the entire day the whale swims an erratic course back and forth in front of the house. Three times I lose sight of him, only to have him reappear within forty-five minutes. I listen all day, but he never makes a sound. I spend the day watching him and standing in my slippers next to the warm wood stove. I record the time between each of his breaths. I have never seen a whale remain in one place for so long. It feels strange to be conducting killer whale research so comfortably on such a wet and windy day.

Lone killer whales are very rare and to date they have always been transient males. Transients typically have smaller families and on occasion a female must die leaving only one male offspring. Having no sister or tight bond with an aunt, these males wander from pod to pod and on occasion travel alone. I name this fellow Numas after a solitary island.

30 January

0830 — Still in bed, I glance out the window. Unbelievably, Numas is still out in front of my house! The weather has settled down, so I go out with him. I keep telling myself he is not waiting for me, but it sure feels like he is.

1400 — I spend the day with Numas, watching him hunt the coastline north of my place. I see no sign that he is successful and at 1445 I have to leave to pick up Jarret from school.

Where Do Whales Go in the Winter?

Some whales migrate in the winter, like humpback and Gray whales, which go south to have their babies. While there isn't much food for them in Mexico and Hawaii, their calves apparently need the warmer water to survive their first few months of life. Killer whales don't migrate in the same way, but they do move into different areas of the coast. When the salmon are no longer close to shore travelling towards their streams in huge numbers, the fish-eating whales cannot find food as easily. So they spread out.

In the summer many pods get together. Sometimes we even get superpod days where a hundred whales are all in one area. But in the winter they must eat fish that live on the bottom or in the kelp and these fish don't travel in huge schools. As a result a place that can feed fifty whales in the summer may only be able to feed ten in the winter. Whales don't usually stay in one place during the winter, so they don't eat all the fish living there. They keep travelling, snacking, all the while leaving plenty of fish behind to maintain the population.

Transient whales are more common to see than resident whales during the winter. Their food — seals, sea lions and porpoises — are here year-round. So why don't the transients stay here all year? Because they would eventually run out of food. Instead of eating everything in one place and then moving on, they continuously cruise hundreds of miles eating wounded or weak marine mammals. By doing this they always have food and they don't kill off the healthy and strong animals that keep the population in good shape.

Spring

22 April

<u>1031</u> — Spot transients Innis and her sons, Arrow and Spiller, on my way to drop off the mail at our floating post office. They are travelling south, spread out in hunting formation.

<u>1110</u> — I shut down to listen. They are silent as is usual when they are hunting, but I hear three sea lions breathe in a bay to my left.

<u>1112</u> — Arrow must have heard them too and he drifts towards the bay quietly. Somehow his mother and brother know to join him, although I didn't hear him call. It is possible that he used a frequency above my hearing range or made a noise I didn't attribute to him. Human hunters learned to use bird calls to communicate to each other without being detected. Maybe whales have also learned to disguise their communication. Anything is possible; I just have to become a better observer to find the answers.

<u>1116</u> — Attack! The bay erupts into white water. In the confusion I see a flash of dorsal fin, then a bit of a sea lion's brown fur-clad back, then the three whales and three Stellars are gone.

<u>1119</u> — The sea lions reappear in a tight group bobbing straight up in the water, their necks stretched high. As they snake their heads around looking for the whales, they remind me of Medusa from the Greek myths, who had snakes for hair. No whales in sight.

<u>1122</u> — The sea lions hear the whales blow before I do and the three heads swing in one direction and stare. Innis, flanked by her sons, is heading south fast. The sea lions may have bitten a whale, or perhaps the whales were simply testing them and found them too strong. Making a living isn't always easy for a whale.

Sea Lions

My husband, Robin Morton, dove with killer whales, sharks and many other marine animals, and the only ones that he found frightening and unpredictable were the Stellar sea lions. They pushed at his face mask and grabbed his fins and he felt that they were often more aggressive than playful. They are the largest of the sea lion species and are equipped with a big set of teeth. But as fierce as they are, they appear to be slowly disappearing from the coast and so far scientists don't know why.

When animals start disappearing, no one knows at first if they are getting sick with a deadly disease, if their source of food is disappearing, if they are being poisoned, if the place they have their babies has been disrupted, or if any number of other things have gone wrong. Scientists have to become detectives looking for a killer, and they have to work fast to find these answers, before too few of the species are left. The more we know, the more we can help. Many people studying wild animals today are involved in protecting them because they are the ones who know what has gone wrong.

Killer Whale Games

One thing that I know for sure about killer whales is that they don't always do the same things. I often see a behaviour for a few months and then it is gone. One example of this was one spring when the young males were doing what I named the Angel Stroke. They lay on their backs at the surface and swept their pectoral fins up and down, while splashing with their tails. I saw lots of this in 1985 and thought it must be some kind of courtship behaviour. But I haven't seen it again. Was it a fad?

While I was studying the captive whales in California, I saw play behaviours like this come and go. The most spectacular one I named the Double Layout. I watched the two whales work on it until they were good at it and then they quit! It involved both whales and they had to lay their flukes on the platform, roll a bit to one side and raise their right pectoral fins. While they were learning, one whale would slip off the ledge while the other was just lining up. Or they might turn in opposite positions and bump.

When they got good at it, they just swam up to the platform and did a quick and perfect job. I snapped a picture and showed it to the trainers. They were amazed — getting the two whales to do anything together was very difficult. I wonder, did one whale think of it and teach the other? Or did they make it up as they went along? Why would the whales work on perfecting a behaviour and then stop doing it? Was the "fun" in the learning?

The double layout

23 April

<u>1130</u> — A vessel calls me about whales spotted twenty minutes south of my place. When I arrive, I find Licka, her family and her nephews, Top Notch and Foster. It is like seeing old friends again, their presence hinting that it will soon be summer again. I drop the hydrophone and listen to their calls echoing in the little passage. Resident whales are so much noisier than transients. As usual they are working against the tide.

<u>1210</u> — We reach an intersection of three passages. Licka is floating, while the others mill around her.

<u>1214</u> — Out of nowhere more whales suddenly surface. It's Stripe, her two offspring, and a tiny new calf. I am not sure who the calf belongs to.

<u>1232</u> — I am almost close enough to figure out who the new mum is when a boat pulling a floathouse descends on us and I have to move out of the way.

<u>1332</u> — I am amazed! The baby definitely belongs to Stripe! It has been eleven years since her last calf and her oldest son is twenty. Stripe has had at least one other calf, taken from her as a baby in 1969 and put in an oceanarium. This whale, known as Corky, is one of the last surviving captive killer whales from Canadian waters. Corky, one of the first killer whales I encountered when I began my research in California, has lived virtually her whole life without her family, and has watched her babies, mate and other whales in the tank die. There is now an international effort underway to release her back to her family.

Photos were taken during the capture in 1969 and, because Corky swam close to Stripe until they were forced apart, we know that Stripe is her mother. Mothers and babies generally swim together, but, when there is danger or confusion, babies become their mother's little shadow, staying as close as possible. Corky was about five years old when she was captured. The youngest wild whale we know of to give birth was eleven and so that would make Stripe at least forty years old and probably older. Until today no one knew a whale could give birth so late in life.

I am looking forward to making this birth announcement. I name the baby Fife, as the whales turn into a channel by that name.

May you always swim with your family, little whale, and live to become old and wise.